PYROGR

WOOD BURNING

A Pictorial Step By Step Instructional Guide For Beginners And Seniors To Master The Techniques And Art Of Woodburning, Stencils, Projects, Tools, And Kits Including Safety Tips And Tricks

By

Downey K. Davis

TABLE OF CONTENTS

INTRODUCTION

For centuries or for a considerable length of time, the art of pyrography has been around. It is an ancient technique that uses a heated metal pen to burn wood and leave a decorative pattern. Pyrography, also known as wood burning, is a fantastic technique for experienced draftsmen to test their hand in a different medium. The history of craftsmanship dates back to the times of the Egyptians and some African tribes, and in China, it was known as embroidery with a firing pin. Throughout history, artists have been able to express themselves by creatively burning strokes in wood, leather, and even pumpkins.

Even though pyrography can be drilled with any heated metal device, craftsmen can try different things with different tips for present-day wood-burning equipment with an assortment of brush strokes to accomplish various impacts. Solid, soldering iron-like tips allow large, bold lines, while looped tips can create a fine shade. And by applying different pressures, pyrography artists can achieve different tones, from light brown to maroon.

CHAPTER 1

WHAT IS PYROGRAPHY

Pyrography is the freehand craft of designing wood or other materials with burn marks when a heated object, for example, poker is utilized or used in a controlled way. It is otherwise called **wood-burning** or **pokerwork.**

The term means "writing with fire" from the Greek pure (fire) and Graphos (writing). It can be practiced with special modern branding tools or with a fire-heated metal device or even concentrated sunlight with a magnifying lens. Pyrography dates from the 17th century and peaked in the 19th century. In its raw form, it is poker.

A wide range of colors and colors can be achieved. Different effects occur depending on the type of tip used, the temperature, or the way iron is applied to the material. After firing the design, wooden objects are often colored. Light hardwoods such as sycamore, linden, beech, and birch are used most often because their fine grain is not distracting. However, other woods such as pine, oak, or maple are also used. Pyrography is also applied to leather goods using the same hot ironing technique. Leather is suitable for bold designs and also enables very subtle shades. Uncommon vegetable-tanned calfskin or leather ought to be utilized for pyrography (as present-day tanning strategies leave synthetics on the leather that are harmful when consumed), as a rule in a light color for the good difference.

Pyrography is also popular with pumpkin artisans and artists who burn designs on the outside of a dry, hard-shelled pumpkin.

SHORT HISTORY OF PYROGRAPHY

The process has been practiced by various cultures, including the Egyptians and some African tribes since the beginning of recorded history. Pyrograph Robert Boyer suspects that the art form dates back to prehistory when early humans created designs with the charred remains of their fires. It was known in China from the Han Dynasty era when it was known as "Fire Needle Embroidery".

During the Victorian time, the creation of pyrography machines sparked far-reaching enthusiasm for the specialty, and around then the expression "pyrography" begat (earlier the name "pokerwork" was utilized all the more frequently).

In the late nineteenth century, a Melbourne planner named Alfred Smart found that water-based paint can be applied hot to wood by siphoning fuel fumes through a warmed empty platinum stick. This improved the pokerwork process by allowing shades and shades to be added that were previously impossible.

Toward the start of the twentieth century, the advancement of the electric pyrographic hot wire wood etching machine additionally computerized the poker work procedure, and workmanship nouveau pyrographic glove boxes and different works were well known around then.

Pyrography is a traditional folk art in many parts of Europe, including Romania, Poland, Hungary, and Flanders, as well as in Argentina and other areas of South America.

PYROGRAPHIC WOODS QUALITY

Woods differ in **hardness, grain, shape, texture, color**, and **other physical properties.**

1. **Hardness:** All woods can be classified as hard or soft. Conifers are usually conifers (needle blades). When burning in softwood, a little resin may seep out and smell slightly of turpentine.

Hardwoods come from deciduous trees. These hardwood trees can be divided into two different growing seasons (warm and cold season or wet and dry season) each year as:

- **Earlywood:** generally lighter in color and weight and only moderately strong
- **Late Wood:** Generally heavier, darker, and much stronger.

Softwood burns faster than hardwood. Very high temperatures are not required for cooking, just like for hardwoods.

2. **Grain:** The grain is the direction of the fibrous elements of the wood cells. This is important for grinding with the grain. Also, the grain can lead to a deviation from the intended path when using a wooden pencil, unless you apply more pressure and burn more slowly on the grain.

3. **Figure:** This is the natural design or pattern that you can see on the cut surface of the wood. The figure on the wood should always be kept in mind when planning your wood stove.

4. **Texture:** There is a texture on the surface of the wood that feels thick or thin, uniform, or uneven. As a starting wood stove, avoid using very fine or complex designs

on uneven, rough-textured wood. Softwoods are quite thin or moderately thick. For some textures, this may mean you have to compensate for the burn: slower on harder summer wood, faster, and with a lighter touch on softer springwood to achieve overall uniform fire.

5. **Color:** Woodburning should be used primarily to enhance the natural beauty of a wood project. Therefore, don't always hide a beautiful figure, grain, glitter, or color, if there is one.

CHAPTER 2

PYROGRAPHY- FIRST WOODBURNING PROJECT

If you've been thinking about trying this pyrography, it's time to step in!

You have to start somewhere. And the best place to start is where the chances of failure are slim. This charming little project is a great way to test your new hot hobby.

Dwarves live wherever you find a natural environment. If you look closely, you will see signs of windows, doors, and even fireplaces in wild places. I recently sat next to a bark carver who explained his technique of showing the structure of the wood bark house (thanks Steve). Part of the charm of these houses is their unstructured appearance. Virtually everything is crooked, unconventional, and rustic. What a perfect theme for a beginner who is likely to burn crooked, dirty (rustic) lines!

Then let's get started. First, dig up a recording tool. A variable temperature unit with interchangeable pins or tips is preferred. If you only have the old soldering iron units, check if you can find one with a rounded tip and get started.

Choose your wood and sand lightly. Although it can technically be burned on any wood, it is not always recommended to do so. Some woods are too grainy, juicy, too hard, or too soft. My suggestion for beginners is basswood, Italian poplar, aspen, or birch. These woods are evenly grained, smooth, and ensure constant combustion. Start with these and save yourself a lot of trouble. You can attack Pine, Ash, and Yew at any time later if you feel very adventurous or suicidal. (Always research your wood before burning it and take the necessary precautions.

Some woods, such as yew, are poisonous.)

Draw or find a pattern. Transfer your pattern to the wood and prepare to burn. Set up your burner and attach a pen or pen. I use a Collwood B2 pen.

STEP BY STEP INSTRUCTIONS
Step 1: Get Used To Your Pen

Use A Piece Of Wood To Practice.

There are three basic types of markings that you use to engrave this design. They are lines, curves, and doodles in the shade.

You have to experiment with temperature, pressure, and speed until you find the combination that is right for you here are some broad tips that can help...

1. Push the pen over the wood with very light pressure. This gives your lines a clean look.
2. Too much pressure or hesitation will burn holes in your wood (stained).
3. Slow down, a steady and even flow will give your burns a constant color.
4. "Land" your boom like an airplane and "take off like an airplane". This will keep your pen moving and

reduce the likelihood of stains due to hesitation.

5. Adjust your heat so that the speed is comfortable for you. You may need to adjust your warmth for lighter and darker areas during the project.

6. Don't practice for more than 15 minutes ... more than that and you're wasting time ... get to work!

I usually start students with a pen (you can also use a writer). This pen is very forgiving and offers a short learning curve for recording. After you get used to this pen, you have the basic "feeling" of burning yourself and being ready to move on to other pens. This is also a very versatile pen that can be used for a variety of projects.

With these techniques, you should stay away from sharp or razor-sharp pens. You can continue to run this project, but you need to adjust the technique.

Step 2: Start Burning Your Project

First, put on the contours. Don't attack the detail lines yet. Due to the nature of this topic, you can get away with crooked lines. That is why it is such a perfect beginner pattern.

Step 3: Complete The Tree Bark Texture

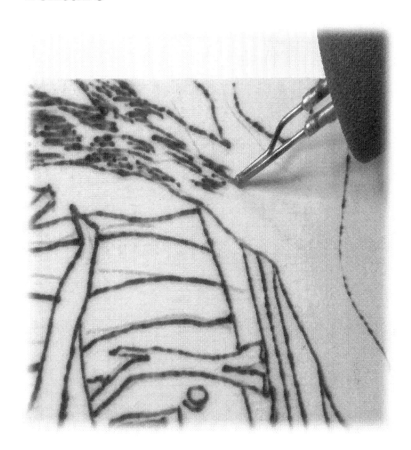

Dwarves or Gnomes like to live in or around trees. So if you burn into the bark, use masses of direction lines. To do this, place several length lines parallel to each other until you get the desired shape.

Be sure to follow the direction of the branches when creating your lines.

Step 4: Finish The Tree

When you've added the bark lines, shade the entire branch with a tight swirl stroke.

Turn down the heat so you don't lose all the details that you've just burned. This is important because we want the viewer to focus on the house. If the detail in the trees is too sharp, it will compete with your center of interest. Subtle shades weaken details.

Step 5: Burn In The Dark Shadows

Increase the heat and use the same swirl stroke that you used for the branches to burn off the darkest shadows.

Step 6: More Dark Surfaces

Fill the eaves and shade the windows with direction marks.

I used a vertical line for the windows and the door and an angled line for the eaves. Angles reinforce what the viewer sees.

Step 7: Burn Into The Liner

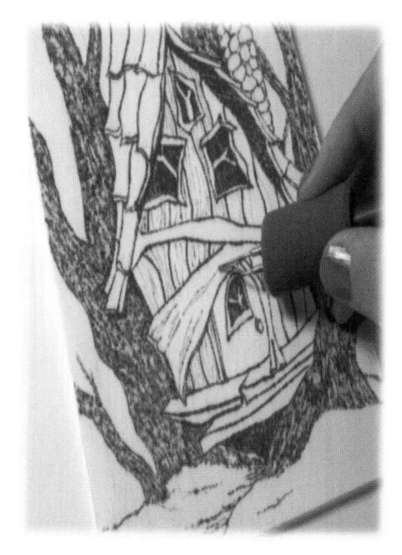

Now turn down the heating and fill the cladding details with clear lines.

Step 8: Burn The Tiles

Add details to the shingles by dragging the lines down from where the shingles overlap.

Don't burn them completely, let them fade smoothly. They have to be irregularly long to have a natural look.

Step 9: Middle Shadow Areas

Now add the lighter shades with the swirl technique and little heat.

Step 10: Personalization With Details

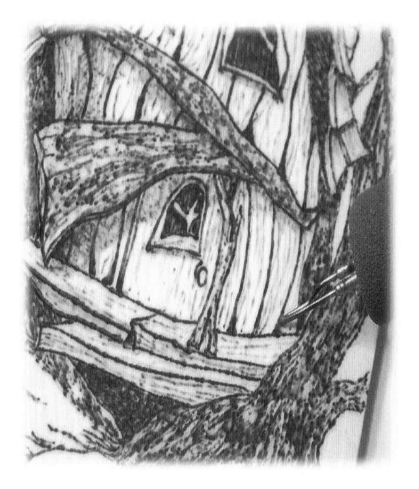

Now you can add some final details. Part of the charm of these little houses is their sloppy looks. Not all tables match, so add random spaces and shade them.

Step 11: Crack Tiles

The tiles may also have cracks at the edges. Have fun adding some cracks.

Step 12: Adding The Stones To The Fireplace

Shade the fireplace stones with the same swirl stroke. Apply shading to the left and bottom of each stone to create a three-dimensional feel.

Take a step back and evaluate your work. Feel free to optimize all areas according to your wishes. You had a good start. Sign your work, find it, and show it!

CHAPTER 3

2020 WOOD BURNING TOOLS AND PYROGRAPHY PENS

In 2020, wood-burning tools and pyrography pens were reviewed. They are as followed below:

1. Burnmaster HAWK Single Port Woodburner PACKAGE

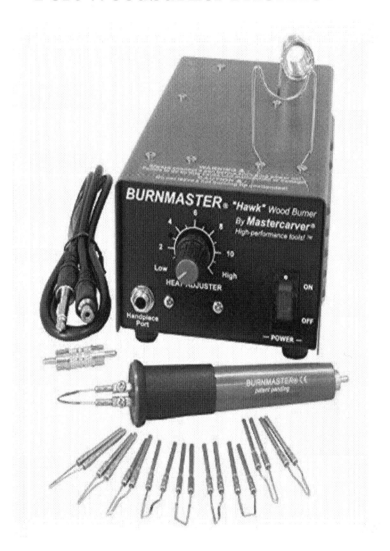

Art in any form can turn an ordinary item into a treasure that you will cherish forever!

The wooden spoon you use to roast vegetables?

Did you know that there is a way to make the spoon more interesting by drawing a simple pattern on the handles?

This personalized touch for kitchen accessories not only brings you some compliments from your family members but also gives you a safer feeling for your work and inspires you to take on more hobbies in the future!

To get you started on the right foot, we'd like to introduce the Woodburner Burnmaster HAWK single-port kit, which contains all the important information a beginner needs to start burning right away.

The Hawk control unit has an output of 130 watts that can be adapted to your needs using the variable micro-heat supply.

Simply turn the heat control knob and choose any number between 1 and 10 that is required for your project.

While it may take a while for the other burners on the market to heat up, it will prepare to rock as soon as you plug it in!

Although it gets a little warm when you use it at its maximum setting all the time, there is a "reset breaker" that switches the device off automatically if it gets too hot for a long period of time.

Highlighted Features:

1. The Hawk kit contains 10 pen tips that are easy to change.
2. The 130-watt unit has an adjustable knob for your convenience.

3. The device has a microcircuit that resets the device if it gets too hot.
4. It heats up as soon as you plug it in.
5. The cable is designed so that it doesn't get in your way while you work.

2. Drtulz 56PCS Wood Burning Kit

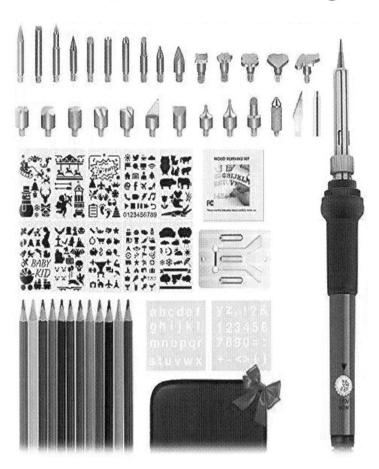

Is your grandfather still wriggling with his old branding tools?

We all know what grandparents are like! They have one thing in common and the tendency is never to throw away old things!

Here's an idea.

Let's make this Christmas season even more special by giving her the new Drtulz firewood kit that contains 56 PIECES of accessories to keep your grandpa busy all day!

The reason why I recommend this kit as an ideal gift is that it contains a lot of new tools, crayons, and many other surprises in its box.

If you look at the device, you will notice that there is a dial that allows you to set the temperature between 200 and 450 degrees Celsius. The device heats up in just 15 seconds after the switch is turned on.

This kit contains the best branding pen that comes with a temperature-resistant housing to protect your fingers from prolonged work.

With 28 different interchangeable pen tips, you can do a variety of activities, including B. Image transfer, cutting templates, welding, stamping, etc.

Note that you must let the device cool down a little by switching off the device before changing another tip.

Not only will it be easy for you to remove the tips this way, but you will also enjoy a longer lifespan.

Highlighted Features:

1. It is a suitable gift to surprise your loved ones.

2. It comes with a variable temperature that can go up to 450 degrees Celsius.
3. The device heats up in 15 seconds after connection.
4. There are 28 different tips to choose from.
5. It can be used to cut stencils, emboss, or emboss fabrics.

3. Truart Level 2 Single Pen Professional Wood Burning Tool

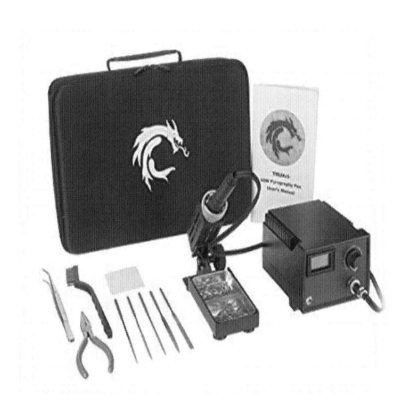

So far we have talked about what a beginner needs when he first enters the world of woodworking.

However, we also have some professionals who are already familiar with the basics and are now looking for something special to add glamor to their work.

To relieve the itching, TRUArt presents a single-stage firewood firing set that has been specially developed for professional craftsmen to meet your requirements.

With an output of 60 watts, this device warms up quickly after switching on and reaches its full potential in a matter of seconds. Above all, the pen is constructed in such a way that it does not heat up even when used with the highest performance!

The Stage 2 version contains 40 different tips that include some unique patterns such as hatching, razors, etc. The package also includes a cleaning pad to polish the tips after you're done with your logging session.

Did you know that brass tips break or dent if you apply too much heat or pressure to them?

With the TRUArt Professional Kit version, you get a digital voltage control with which you can change the temperature in a second!

This is the best firewood set that works with more precision and whose tips have a longer useful life.

Highlighted Features:

1. It comes with 40 different interchangeable tips.
2. Digital voltage control measures temperature accurately.
3. The device responds immediately to the temperature controller.

4. The tips cool in seconds and can be changed quickly.

5. It is mainly suitable for professional wood burners.

4. Colwood Super Pro II Wood BurningKit

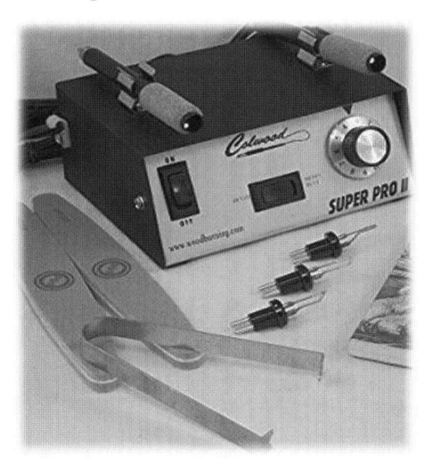

Are you looking for the perfect anniversary gift for your partner?

How about a wooden vase with a big heart?

And don't forget to write both your initials and some romantic lines along the way! Well, we will not go into details anymore and we will leave the rest to your imagination!

To start this thoughtful gesture, you first need a wood kit like Colwood Super Pro II, which includes a writing tip and a popular pyrography workbook by Sue Walters.

Colwood starts positive by including 2 pens in your kit.

The advantage of a dual pen mode is that you can work faster and not have to wait for your pen to cool down while changing its tip.

You can use a toggle switch on the device to decide which pin should be heated first.

This kit includes a tilt, a round bar, and a writing tip that you can use to draw different patterns on your chosen piece of wood.

Although you can choose the wood you prefer, wood burning is usually best for soft textured woods like cedar, pine, poplar, cherry, and basswood.

To extend the life of the pencil tips, use the polishing tip polisher provided with the kit to clean them as soon as you finish making them.

Highlighted Features:

1. The package contains a popular pyrography book.
2. You can work faster with dual pen mode than with a single version.

3. It comes with specially designed pen tips for folding letters.
4. The grinding tip polisher helps to effectively clean the tips.

The device cools down in a minute and allows you to work comfortably

5. Walnut Hollow Creative Versa Tool

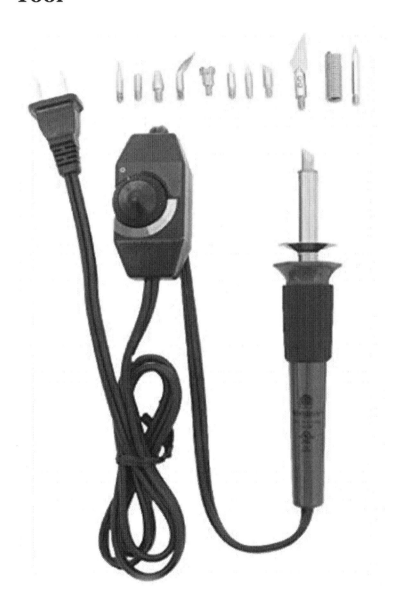

Even if you've never used a hot air gun before, Walnut Hollow's Versa Creative tool makes it easy to learn curves!

This kit was not only specially designed for beginners, but it is also a real bargain in terms of price as it comes with eleven interchangeable points to choose from.

This tool measures 1.7 × 5.3 × 9.8 inches and has a comfortable grip so you can work on your project as long as you want without getting tired. It also comes with a heat shield to protect your fingers in case the device gets too hot for you.

Are you bored if you only see your work on a wooden surface?

Well, I have good news for you!

Walnut Hollow is suitable for working with a variety of materials, such as wood, leather, and cork. And cut and fold each of these materials using its variable temperature control.

Yes! You can control the temperature as you like and flexibly set the range from 0 to 950 degrees Fahrenheit. It is ideal for setting the dial to your preferred point before you start brewing.

Remember the 11 interchangeable tips Hollow promised?

On a positive note, these tips are lead-free solders, which means that using this product can turn GREEN.

These tips are also used for a variety of different styles, including cone, calligraphy, shading, stamping, universal, mini universal, hot knife, flux, mini flux, cone, and weld.

Highlighted Features:

1. It comes with a comfortable handle that can be used for a long time.
2. You can set a temperature between the specified ranges.

3. The device has 11 different interchangeable tips for different styles.
4. It can also be used for other materials.
5. Walnut has added heat resistant protection for your convenience.

6. WAMTHUS Wood Burning kit

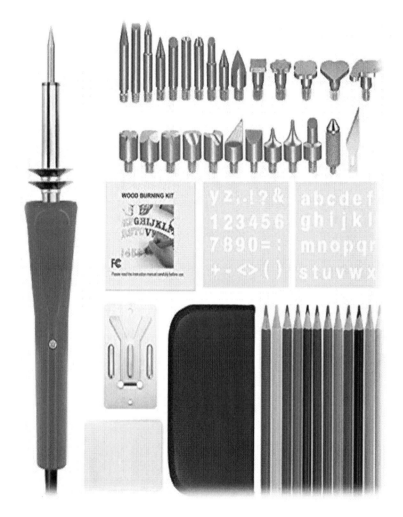

Did you know that your hands can cause severe cramping when you perform jobs that require repeated movements, such as burning wood?

Relax! We obviously don't suggest giving up on your favorite hobby!

Instead, you need to find a suitable device like the WAMTHUS Firewood Kit, which is designed so that you can work at different angles without having to press your hands.

The ergonomically shaped handle is comfortable enough to last a long time, and the best part is that it's quite light!

30-watt soldering machines are bright red in color and are perfect for drilling, cutting, burning, and engraving on various surfaces such as wood, leather, plastic, cloth, and paper.

WAMTHUS offers you many options and allows the user to control everything from scratch.

For example, if you get bored of drawing the same pattern, you can easily change the tips of your device and choose one from the collection of 26 different wood and soldering tips.

Still not live up to your expectations?

Well, the pack also includes 12 crayons to give your art a lively look!

Just outline your favorite design on the board. Then use the kit to engrave it on the wood. Finally, use the colored pencils to bring out the details and make it look alive.

Highlighted Features:

1. The package contains 44 different accessories.
2. You can comfortably draw with the ergonomic handle.
3. The 26 different tips can be easily exchanged while working.
4. The welding machine heats up in just 45 seconds.

5. The kit includes some colored pencils to make your graphics more fun.

7. Truart (Level 1) Wood and Leather Pyrography Pen

When I plan to buy a DIY kit, I first check that the toolkit contains the correct instructions, usage guidelines, and warning signs for safety reasons.

Since I do all the hard work myself, it would be terrible if all my efforts were free for just one simple mistake!

Well, TRUArt seems to meet all of my criteria and includes complete instructions that clearly state how to use this tool properly.

The device itself heats up pretty quickly, so you have enough time to work on multiple projects at the same time.

To keep up with your creative ideas, TRUArt has 21 different interchangeable tips including groove, dot, solder point, razor blade, pattern transfer, stripes, markers, knives, calligraphy, and more.

The best part is that you can tie all of these amazing pattern tips together with a feather that has a heat and impact resistant rubber grip so you can work comfortably.

TRUArt is a multi-purpose tool and works on both wood and leather. In dual power mode, you can operate the device with 15 watts for leather and 30 watts for firewood.

Highlighted Features:

1. The kit includes 21 choices for creating different patterns.
2. It contains detailed instructions and tips for beginners.
3. The pen is light, easy to hold, and heat resistant.
4. In dual power mode, you can work with both wood and leather.
5. It has a quick heating system. 6. The stainless steel construction of the device makes it durable.

8 TAMEHOM wood Burning kit

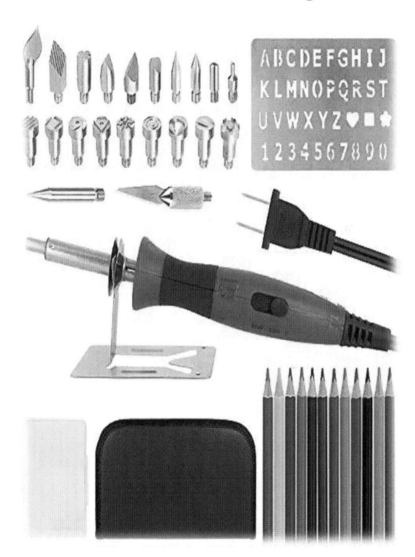

By involving your children in the art of wood-burning, you can discover their artistic skills in a fun and creative way!

For this purpose, you can even use the spare wooden blocks that have been in your room for years! All you need is a high-quality firewood kit to draw your child's attention to this fun but educational activity.

I think it is the perfect time to put our next item on the list, which is a TAMEHOM UL Listed firewood kit.

It has everything you need in one package and is suitable for everyone, be it a pro or a beginner!

TAMEHOM is a multi-purpose tool that can be used for pyrography, welding, leather burning, paper making, stamping, embossing, etc.

Depending on the material you are working on, you can set the temperature of the device, which can be between 400 and 850 degrees Celsius at maximum setting.

Are you out of inspiration? Well, this kit contains lots of supplies to cheer you up!

From templates to various tips for wood embossing, TAMEHOM offers you a complete package with all the important information!

You can also have a knife holder with a blade, 10 soldering tips, 9 wood engraving tips, a stencil, a wooden pen, and a plastic box with a tip holder and a case to carry all of these amazing products inside.

Another good news is that this device comes with a metal bracket that holds and holds the heated device to ensure its safety.

So you can spend as much time as you want with your artwork without being a bit distracted!

Highlighted Features:

1. This kit is suitable for a variety of materials.
2. You can set the temperature between 400 and 850 degrees Celsius.
3. The package contains many accessories for beginners.
4. The red LED display helps you a lot with your fast work.
5. It has a metal bracket that can be used to hold the heated device.

9. Fuyit 42-piece LCD Wood Burning kit

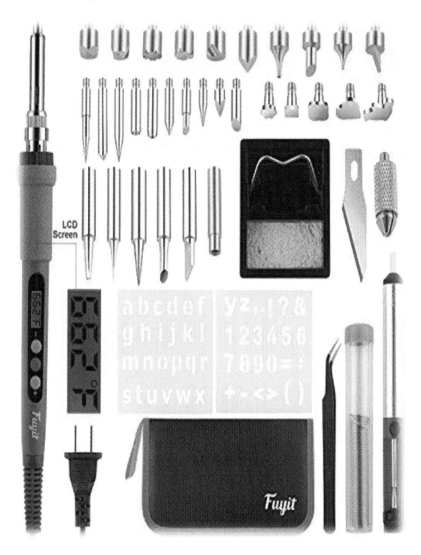

We are all creatures of habit.

Once we find the perfect rhythm that works best for us, we often stay in that comfort zone.

With that in mind, Fuyit has developed a digital pyrographic pen that remembers the temperature he used in his last session and is resumed at the point you turn it on next time. How cool is that

If you move on to accessories, this kit includes 28 different curved tips and 5 soldering tips.

All tips are interchangeable and include a variety of collections, including universal, conical, calligraphic, shaded, transfer, flow, hot knife, and soldering tips.

With all of these accessories, you can use this kit with different materials like leather, cork, foam, solder board, etc. Do not worry!

You can set the temperature between 180 and 480 degrees Celsius to suit your needs for any project that you can easily work on.

Fuyit always strives to use the latest technology and this product is no exception!

Equipped with ceramic technology with internal heating, the pen heats up in 40 seconds and prepares to offer you the best possible experience.

You can control the temperature level using the thermostatic LCD screen connected to the stylus and switch instantly if necessary.

Highlighted Features:

1. The 42-piece kit contains everything for beginners or professional artists.
2. Ceramic technology helps heat the tool in 40 seconds.

3. You can monitor and control the temperature through the LCD screen.
4. The device saves and uses the last configuration it has worked on.
5. Contains 28 curved tips for various purposes.

10. ATHOMEY 40Pcs wood Burning kit

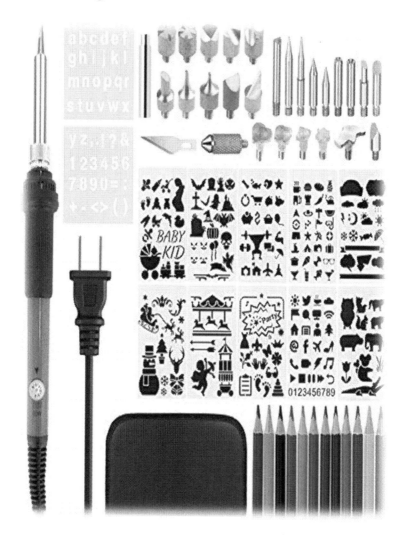

Do you remember the trip to the beach that you did last summer? The shots were great, wasn't it?

While searching for a perfect frame to display those beautiful memories, there is an inexpensive way to give this simple, old, and boring wooden frame a new look with some basic pyrographic skills.

If you are interested in this idea and still don't know where to start, check out the ATHOMEY 40Pcs Wood Burning Kit.

This kit contains everything a beginner needs to know and includes a clear user guide to accompany you on your way!

With 60 watts of power and heated ceramic technology inside, it takes no more than 45 seconds for this device to fully heat up and be ready to use. You can also regulate the temperature between 200 and 450 degrees centigrade.

As a beginner, it is quite understandable if you are a little nervous about leaving your first mark on the board.

To help you with your crafts, ATHOMEY contains 28 soldering tips and accessories that are easy to use and help you complete your first DIY project!

You will also receive a converter, 5 different wood embossing tips, a hot knife holder with a blade, and a carrying case to carry everything inside.

Highlighted Features:

1. The soldering iron is light and compact enough to be used comfortably.
2. It comes with a variable temperature that can be easily adjusted.
3. It only takes 45 seconds to prepare this device for use.
4. With the 28 welding tips, you can work with different styles.
5. It contains clear instructions to accompany you on your way.

CHAPTER4

WOOD BURNING KIT AND HOW IT WORKS

After you've decided to take a look at the world of woodworking, it's time to get a good set of wood-burning tools that contain everything you need to start your first pyrography project right away.

A wood stove set usually comes with a crayon that is heated to draw sketches on a plank, and various solder clips to cut and fold different shapes on it.

TYPES OF WOOD BURNING TOOLS

An artist needs different tools to improvise! When it comes to wood tools, you will find two different categories, described below:

A. CRAFT STYLE

Beginners love craft-style solid-tip tools because they come with larger pen handles. That means you have better control while you work!

It also comes with a thick brass tip that heats up to a preset temperature so you can focus on your project without worrying about the temperature.

Some tools even have a double heat shield to protect your hand from overheating! However, there is also a downside.

This tool is not suitable for fine detailed work. It is best suited to fill large gaps between two edges. It also takes longer to cool the tips of the pen, which takes up to 8 minutes each.

B. WIRE SPRING

Variable temperature wire tip tools are mainly preferred by professionals and advanced users. The handling of these tools is much smaller, making it easier to write a lot with these pens without cramping your hands!

The wire springs cool in a short time thanks to their two-wire elements, usually within one to two minutes. The notable feature is the variable temperature control, which allows you to draw detailed graphics quickly and accurately at the same time.

However, it will take some time to get used to this technique, especially if you are just starting.

FACTORS TO CONSIDER BEFORE BUYING A WOOD BURNING KIT

Do you know the functions that you should pay attention to when buying a Wood Burning Kit?

If not, we are here to give you an idea of what to expect from a high-quality kit and what to avoid so as not to be disappointed with your next purchase.

Let's see!

1. COMFORT

Whether you're working on your DIY projects or just practicing to improve this craft, you're more likely to spend a lot of time holding your utensils.

Therefore, the crayon must be light enough to hold it easily and comfortably for a long period of time.

Also, look for spring with a smaller handle. Not only does it help you work without having a cramp in your hand, but it also allows you to easily draw fine details.

2. ADJUSTABLE PENCIL TIPS

If you are just a beginner, you can use pens with fixed tips at the ends. They tend to heat up in less time and are suitable for a uniform writing style.

However, once you start working with somewhat more complex designs, you'll soon be looking for ways to achieve different effects in your workpiece.

You will need a kit with versatile tips and a spring that can be attached to it.

When purchasing, please make sure the package contains pencil tips that allow for fine and thick lines.

3. EQUIPMENT

Say YES to the free accessories!

As a beginner, you probably haven't prepared anything for your first craft project.

You can buy all the necessary items individually, but wouldn't it be nice if you had them all in one package and for free?

A complete package like this contains many things like stencils, transfer paper, colored pencils for enhanced effects, knife holders with a blade, metal holder, operating instructions for better understanding, and much more!

Choose the package that you think will contain most of the items you need, and be sure to check the price to make sure it fits your budget!

4. RAPID HEATING

I don't know anything about you, but I find it a little inconvenient to sit like an idiot while your tools slowly heat up!

Imagine if you had to participate in several projects at the same time, it would take forever to do your job!

Therefore, you should look for devices that don't take that long and heat up pretty quickly in 2-3 minutes, saving valuable time and energy.

5. TEMPERATURE CONTROL

Some devices have a fixed temperature, others offer you the possibility to adjust the temperature according to your requirements.

Well, you can go either way in this situation. With a fixed temperature device, you can work at rest without checking if it's too hot or not hot enough.

On the other hand, a device with variable temperature offers you more flexibility and the possibility to try out different styles and patterns.

It is recommended to choose this option if you are at a medium to advanced level in the elaboration.

6. POWER

Do not fall into the trap of thinking that the more powerful a wooden feather is, the better it is!

A low-performance ballpoint pen is better for you if you want to draw detailed jobs and have to drive slower.

A strong feather heats up fairly quickly and leaves a black mark there if you hold it too long.

However, if you know what you are doing, you can design fairly quickly and do your job faster. Then a powerful device may be the better choice for you.

Before you start playing and experimenting with designs and patterns, you must first choose which type of wood to draw and which pencil tip is best for this purpose

CHAPTER 5

STEP BY STEP INSTRUCTIONS TO PREPARE WOOD FOR BURNING OR PYROGRAPHY

Prepare the selected wood in advance for your wood-burning session to be successful. Do the following:

1. Choose A Suitable Part

Cut the wood to a size suitable for your project. Then examine the surface to see if it has a small mark.

If you find a dent or two, lay it on the surface with a damp, folded cloth. Then press the fabric with an iron and keep pressing until this point is higher until it is no longer noticeable.

2. Sand Down The Base

You only need 320 grit sandpaper for this purpose.

First, determine in which direction the wood fiber is pointing. Then use the sandpaper to polish the surface as much as possible while moving it in the same direction to avoid scratches on the surface.

Then use a small towel to remove all the sawdust from the board.

3. Wet The Wood

After completely sanding the board, it's time to bathe it!

Well, we are not going to let the surface drain completely! It is intended to moisten the surface enough to remove all dust on the surface. You can use a damp sponge for this purpose.

4. Make It Smooth!

After the plank has dried, it is best to sand it carefully again. The surface should now be really smooth.

And now your piece of wood is ready for all kinds of recording sessions! You can see our simple firewood art ideas.

HOW TO USE A WOOD BURNING TOOL

Once you have purchased a wood-burning tool, the rest of the steps are easy if you follow the instructions below.

1. Choose Your Favorite Tip

Most of the wood kit contains multiple pencil tips including Universal, Conical, Transfer, Shading, Flow, Calligraphy, etc.

The first thing to do is to select the tip you want to work with and install it on the welding machine. Then insert the tips into the head of the device and continue to rotate it until it clicks into place.

Watch out! Do not try to tighten it firmly with pliers, as too much pressure can cause the tip to break completely.

2. Use A Template If Necessary

Some kits contain multiple templates that you can use to create different patterns if you're a little intimidated to burn the first time you try!

The template technique is quite simple. Simply place the template on the chosen wood and trace the design with the help of a pencil.

There! You now have the advantage that your piece of wood has a pre-drawn pattern that can be easily traced later.

3. Connect The Device

Depending on the model of your tool, you may need to find an outlet that meets the voltage requirements of the device.

After connecting, you may have to wait a while for the device to heat up to the correct temperature. The waiting time can vary from a few seconds to a maximum of 8 minutes.

4. Start Burning!

Once the device has fully warmed up, it's time to cast your spell and show your magic!

Yes! Now is the time to develop your artistic skills in wood and enjoy the view of your burnt design on the board.

5. Change Tips If You Want

If you are bored and want to try a different pattern, replace the installed tip with another one.

However, you must turn off the device and let it cool down first. Then try to unhook the tips by hand and use pliers only when necessary.

6. Mark The Parts With Colored Pencil

When you're done recording the design, you can look at your work and feel something missing!

Well, for color-loving people, some manufacturers have included colored pencils in their kit.

You can add a little color to your project and highlight the parts you want to give it.

TYPES OF WOOD AND HOW THEY WORK

No two types of wood achieve the same effect! It is therefore important that you choose your favorite canvas according to your requirements.

Although there are several other options, here we will talk about those that are suitable for beginners.

i. PINE

Pinewoods have a smooth texture that makes it easy to create different patterns, grooves, and raised lines. The light brown color makes it easy to shine your drawing, and the best part is that it's pretty cheap!

ii. MAPLE

You can find this in every general timber store. Maples have a perfect balance and do not tear, even if your tool slips and burns too much while working. It has a light to medium shade.

iii. POLAR

Polar is a cheaper version of Maple, but it works just as well! The plank is furrow-resistant, making it easier to fix a bug. It comes in the right shade and is available in various sizes at any local craft store.

iv. BASSWOOD

Basswood's bright and light color makes it perfect for beginners. It contains minimal grain, is smooth like butter, and easy to draw decorative patterns. However, it is slightly more expensive than the Polar.

TYPES OF PENS

Once you've unpacked your firewood kit, you'll find various tips with different styles waiting for you to try them on!

Let's look at some of the basic pen advice for beginners:

i. UNIVERSAL ADVICE

The universal tip has a fine, sharp edge with which fine, medium, or thick lines can be drawn depending on the position of the pyrography pen. You can also try holding it at a different angle to easily get the result you want.

ii. FLOW ADVICE

If you want a smooth tip that glides effortlessly across the surface, this is the one for you. A flow tip has a round shape and is also used to draw moles.

iii. CALLIGRAPHY ADVICE

It is very similar to the universal tip and can easily be used to create calligraphy-style lettering. You can draw fine or thick lines as desired.

In addition to these, there are other tooltips to choose from, including tapered tips, hatch tips, marker tips, slot tips, transfer tips, point tips, and stamp tips, etc.

However, you need to learn different techniques to use them properly.

TIPS FOR BURNING WOOD: SAFETY COMES FIRST

Before you start burning your chosen wood frame, you should first practice a bit of scrap metal.

1. Allow the tip of the pencil to cool down as you exchange it for another.
2. After a cooking session, clean the tips properly to avoid carbon buildup.
3. Use light wood to highlight the colors of your workpiece.
4. To start with a good grade, try blowing up when you first touch the wood.
5. If the wood you choose is grainy, apply more heat to burn in these areas.
6. Start with light, smooth strokes, then progress to deeper strokes for the best result.

CHAPTER 6

HOW TO WOOD-BURN ART

In this chapter, I will show you how to take a picture and engrave it by hand on a piece of wood. As an example, I used the heraldic lion of the house Lannister from the book / TV series "Game of Thrones".

STEP BY STEP

Step 1: Deliveries

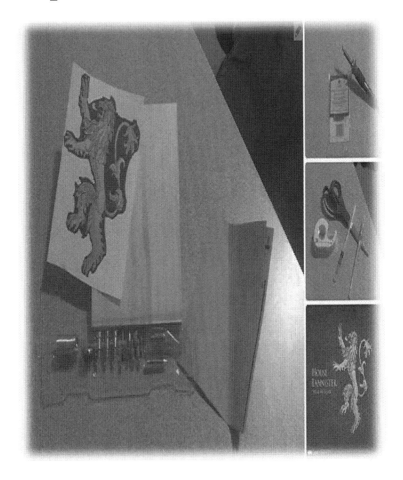

- ➢ Wood, cut (I prefer the use of pine. It is soft enough to burn, but not too soft like linden)
- ➢ 320 grit sandpaper
- ➢ Pyrography pen

- Graphite transfer paper
- Color pencil
- Scissors
- headband
- A picture of burning wood

Step 2: Prepare The Wood

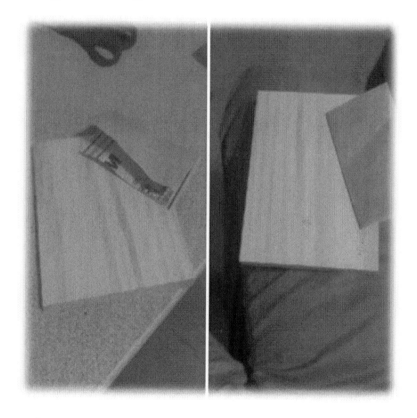

When you have cut your piece of wood, check it to make sure it has no dents or marks. If you find relatively shallow dents or dents, just take a damp cloth, fold it at least once and place it over the flaws. Then press the washcloth with a hot iron. Continue this process until the dents in the wood are raised. Let the wood dry.

Now take your sandpaper and sand the wood to a nice smooth finish. I would recommend wrapping the sandpaper around a flat block of wood to make sure you get a smooth surface.

Step 3: Transfer The Image (for those of us who can't draw freehand)

Once the wood is finished, prepare your image as desired and print it. I made a simple photoshop just to remove the background and save ink. Cut the graphite paper with the image and glue it. Be sure to put the transfer side down.

Pick up your colored pencil and simply draw on the image (see image 4). Check only the parts you want to transfer to the wood. I would recommend not tracking the areas you want to shade.

Step 4: Voila!

Carefully lift your image/graphite paper and see the fruits of your labor. At this point, look at your image on the wood and check for any unwanted marks (image 3). Do not worry! Take sandpaper and carefully sand any stain (picture 3).

Step 5: Security And Technology

Choose the correct pen tip (image 2) and let the pen warm up.

SAFETY

1. Provide adequate ventilation (open window/fan)
2. A clean, open workplace with nothing flammable nearby
3. Coldwater and emergency burn ointment

TECHNIQUES

1. The "flat" side of the tip is mainly used for thick lines, smoothly curved lines, and shadows (figure 3).
2. B) The "blade" side of the tip is used for fine detail (image 4). This can cause very deep burns to the wood if you are not careful.

Note that it takes a lot of practice to master it. I have been there for almost 2 years and even still ruin it!

Step 6: First Burns

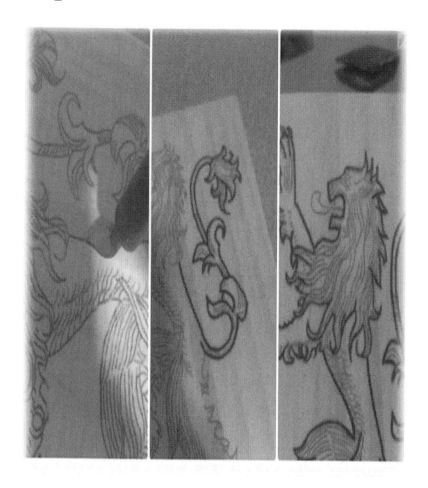

After learning about the technology, the easiest way to start the recording process. In the lion example, the back and tail are mainly flat baselines (Figure 2).

Continue with the rest of the basic lines. It gets easier, trust me.

TUNNEL VIEW

With this burn, I noticed that it is easy to lose track of where you are working. This may be the case if you engage in more complex parts of the job. For example, I had to stop and think while working on the part where the mane overlapped my arm (image 3).

Step 7: The Details

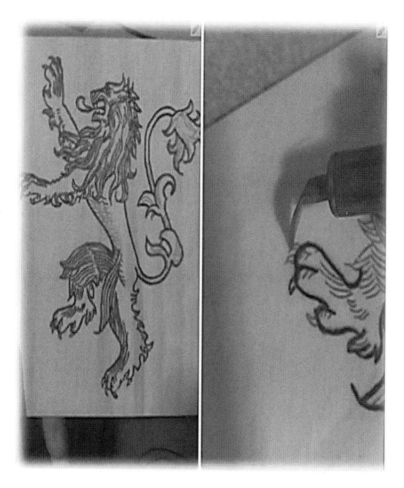

When you have finished the main lines, it is up to you how to proceed. Some images require a lot of detail, others less. The most important part of the details is being slow. Concentrate on certain parts at the same time (for example, the mane, an arm).

Without a video and time-lapse, it's hard to show you the detailed work but think about the technique where the "blade side" of the spring is used for small details (image 2).

A word of caution when using pine wood: You will notice the light and dark spots on the grain. The lightest is the softest wood. If you have to burn in a darker part of the grain (figure 1), you will see that it does not burn as easily. You should carefully walk the same line until it is dark enough to match the rest of the job.

Step 8: Preparing For Shading

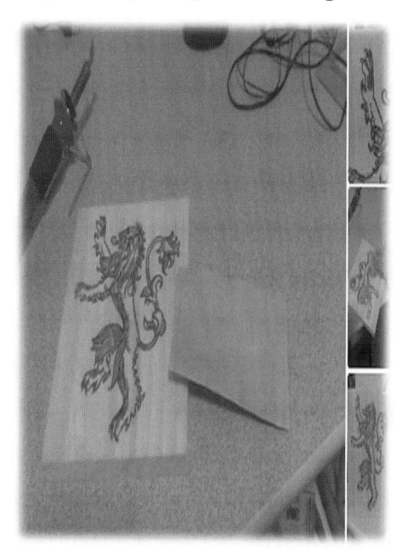

When you are done with the baseline and details, A) compliment yourself and B) prepare your work for shading.

Parts at work may not exactly match the graphite trace (image 2). Do not worry! Take your sandpaper (320 grit or higher) and sand the entire piece lightly. This removes flat burns and traces of graphite.

Clean the wood from the sawdust and be sure to remove it from all lines. You want a nice clean piece to shade.

Step 9: Shading, Part 1

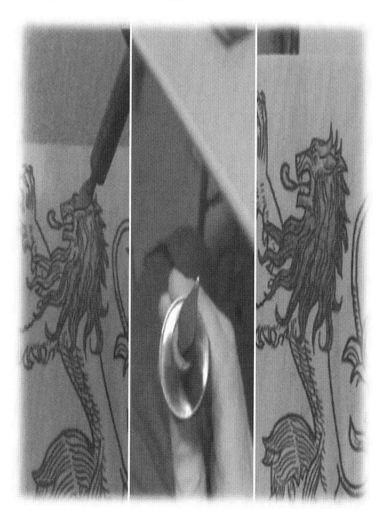

Adding shadows to your work really reinforces it and can also help add depth. But I also have to warn you that it is the most difficult part and requires some experience.

First, decide where you want to donate shade (lion's mane). Second, determine how dark it should be and whether you want to change the shading in different parts (gradient). When asked how dark it is, I would say that the darker should not hide its baseline and detail lines (image 1).

HOW TO SHADE

Use the same spring that you used for the lines (picture 2). I use the end of this pen which is flat and about 1mm wide. Hold the pen as a flat line and just touch the top of the wood. While holding it on the wood, move your hand in a circle and keep the tip at the same angle. You should notice that the wood begins to darken. Keep doing this until you have reached the desired wood tone.

Keep moving the tip. If you let them sit in one place for too long or prefer some of the wood over the other, this becomes visible. In this case, try mixing the darker parts into the lighter parts.

Step 10: Shading, Part 2

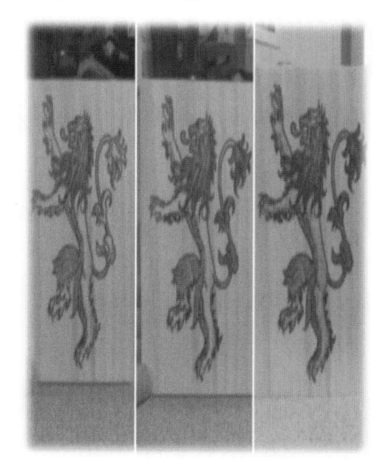

Shades are a great way to add depth to your job. You can turn an average job into something surprising.

I will use my lion work as an example.

After shading the mane, I still found the work too boring. I noticed that two other points were the main candidates for additional shades: the feathers on the tail and the fur hanging on the legs and arms. I shadowed them in the same darkness as the mane (picture 2).

To give it a nice touch, I decided to lightly shade the rest of the lion's body so that it was defined against the normal wood background.

The important part of this is mixing the darker parts with the rest of the light body. This does not apply to the mane, as it is "separated" from the body, but to the tail feathers and the leg/arm hair.

Tip: If you are wrong about shading or just want to get lighter, don't be afraid to lightly sand over problem areas with sandpaper.

Step 11: Done!

After you're done shading, you're done with your work! Take a step back and appreciate the hard work you've put into it. Don't forget to add your own brand to the piece, either on the front like a painting or on the back (Image 2).

At this point, you can leave the wood unchanged or protect it. Polyurethane, oil, paint, wood stain all work. A word of caution about these methods: For example, if you use a dark spot, the shading may be less pronounced.

CHAPTER 7

PYROGRAPHY PROJECTS
step-by-step instructions
project:

A. Carousel Horse Wood Burning

Let's go through a firewood project step by step so you can see how a design is created.

Step 1:

Do you need your wooden tool, a 9? x 12? empty linden wood, an enameled tile on which the tool rests, sandpaper, tracing paper, watercolor pencils, adhesive tape, and polyurethane spray seal.

Grind the project board thoroughly before you begin the recording steps. Remove dust by wiping with a clean cloth

Rub the back of the sample paper with the tip of a soft pencil. Glue the pattern onto the project board and draw over the design lines.

Once the pattern has been transferred to the wood, you can pass the pattern lines with your pencil to darken them as needed.

Step 2:

Start with the wooden side of the tools to shade the horse's body. Note here that the two hind legs burn a little darker than the foreground legs. The abdominal area also has additional darkness.

The central areas of the individual body parts have been left in the natural wood tones. This gives the horse around feeling.

Step 3:

Use the blade edge of the wooden tool to sketch the horse's body. Rotate the tool between your thumb and index finger to curl the lines.

Step 4:

The horse's mane and tail, as well as its saddle, bridles, and accents, were shaded. Use the side tool. Change the color of the hatch as you work. Some areas can have very dark shadows, while others can have a lighter shadow. This increases interest in the job.

Step 5:

The details of the mane, tail, saddle, bridle, and accents were made. Study the horse's close-up photo for ideas on how each was accomplished.

Step 6:

The color can easily be added with colored pencils on burned wood patterns. I used watercolor pencils that are applied like any other colored pencil, except that they can then be mixed with a small amount of water on a soft brush. This blending step removes any remaining lines from the penciling job.

Since the pencil has a solid, solid tip, only the top of the burn is colored so that all the details and shadows of the wood are preserved.

After coloring is complete, give the piece several light coats of a polyurethane spray sealer according to the manufacturer's instructions.

B. Ceremonial Mask Pyrography Project

Ceremonial and ritual masks use strong patterns of geometric lines and abstract shapes to create facial features and express emotions that are prohibited from the myths and legends of culture. They are often carved out of wood with open holes for the mask's eyes and mouth. Raffia, dried reeds, walnuts, seed pods, and even shells can decorate the geometric patterns of the mask or surround the outer edge of the wooden mold. Animal hair and fur have been added in the past to enhance the human or animal impressions they represent.

Burning Supplies:

- Cooking unit with variable temperature.
- Ball tip or loop pin
- Spear Shader Feather
- curved shader pin

Pyro Blank Wood:

- 9 "x 9" poplar exercise chart
- 9 "x 9" Poplar Precut Heart

Pyro Pen detergent:

- Leather belts
- Routing connection
- 1500 grit emery cloth

General:

- 220 or 320 grit sandpaper
- clean dry duster
- Graphite paper
- No. 2 to No. 4 soft pencil
- rule
- Masking tape or painter's tape
- 8 "square brown paper bag

Optional finishing accessories:

- Watercolor paints
- Watercolor crayons
- Polyurethane spray or acrylic sealant

C. American Hero WoodBurning Project

This project is carried out with a heated wood tool and interchangeable brass tips.

Deliveries:

- A wood tool with a temperature
- Standard writing tip
- oval 9? x 12? 3/4? Basswood plate
- Transparent paper
- soft pencil number 2
- 220 grit sandpaper

Step 1

Sand your Linde badge lightly with 220 grit sandpaper. Process the sandpaper with the wood grain to avoid scratches when sanding. Wipe the board with a soft, dry cloth to remove dust.

Make a copy of the pattern. Rub the back of the pattern paper with a # 2 soft pencil and completely cover the pattern areas. Center the pattern on the front of the plate and glue it in place. Use an ink stick along the lines of the pattern. The pencil-rubbed graphite on the back of the pattern leaves a gray line on your dash.

Step 2

Wood tools with temperature reach a temperature setting: hot. Hot temperatures create dark, black lines of fire. To control the tonal values of your shot with a one-temperature tool, you can start shooting before the tip has reached its maximum temperature.

If you burn shortly after inserting your tool, you will get pale tone lines. The tip of the tool continues to heat up as you work. Therefore, move your work to the value ranges for the mid-tone. With a little more time, the tool reaches its full settings and you can edit the dark tones.

To return to pale values, disconnect the plug from the socket and let the device cool down for about five minutes. Then the process begins again. Due to this method of initiating cold burns in the dark area, it is often easier to edit a small area of the project pattern and edit all the tonal values in that area.

step 3

Using textures as fill patterns can also increase the tonal range of a wood-burning tool project with a temperature. Textures do not completely fill a burn area; Allow some burnt lines and some rough wood within the texture line. Tight textures produce dark chocolate colors, medium wrap textures produce a wide range of mid-tones and fine lines with lots of raw wood that form the light areas of your design.

FREQUENTLY ASKED QUESTIONS ABOUT THE WOOD BURNING TOOL

1. How do I avoid getting the tips of the pen dirty?

Answer: Over time, dirt and carbon can of course accumulate on your pen tips. To remove this, you can use a sharpening tool or sandpaper to remove dirt and small particles.

2. How can wood art be kept for a long time?

Answer: Sunlight is the main reason that your artwork loses color over time. To protect your work, it is a good idea to use a protective varnish for your finished project.

3. Do pyrography tools produce smoke?

Answer: Yes. While the wood is burning, it is natural to feel a little smoke and a burning smell while working. You can fix this by installing a desktop fan to blow the air out of your workstation.

4. Can I draw on my leather jacket with wooden tools?

Answer: This is probably a bad idea. Most leather jackets are chrome-tanned and therefore contain chromium ions, which release harmful chemicals when burned.

However, you can use the pyrography tools in vegetable-tanned jackets because they pose no such risks and are safe to use.

5. How can I correct an incorrectly drawn pattern?

Answer: Be careful before drawing in the forest. If you make a mistake, use a sharp tool such as a metal blade or scraper and scrape off the burned parts as much as possible.

6. Can I burn painted wood?

Answer: NO! Burning wood that has been painted, altered, treated, filtered, or modified in any way should always be avoided as it tends to release a harmful chemical into our environment.

Buying freshly cut wood in the store will cost you little. In this case, do not try to use a shortcut method.

CONCLUSION

One thing that distinguishes pyrography from other crafts is that it requires relatively fewer tools.

However, the feeling of satisfaction that you feel after completing a project is immense and motivates you to further advance your rewarding hobby.

In fact, many people have turned their desire to work with wood into a profitable business by creating decorative pieces, signs, pictures, or custom frames and selling them for a good amount of money.

So what are you waiting for?

Get the best wood burning instrument in your assortment and begin burning immediately!

Regardless of your skills and how well your piece turns out, one thing is certain, you will have a lot of fun playing with different tips, textures, and more depth for your work!

Printed in Great Britain
by Amazon

56548093R00076